NOV 0 5 2021

Albany Public Library
Albany, NY

animal planet™

I Am Major
★ **First Dog** ★
Level 2

MAJOR

D1512075

Written by Brenda Scott Royce
Illustrated by Adam Devaney

Silver Dolphin

PRE-LEVEL 1: ASPIRING READERS

 LEVEL 1: EARLY READERS

 LEVEL 2: DEVELOPING READERS

- Simple factual texts with mostly familiar themes and content
- Concepts in text are supported by images
- Includes glossary to reinforce reading comprehension
- Repetition of basic sentence structure with variation of placement of subjects, verbs, and adjectives
- Introduction to new phonic structures
- Integration of contractions, possessives, compound sentences, and some three-syllable words
- Mostly easy vocabulary familiar to kindergarteners and first-graders

 LEVEL 3: ENGAGED READERS

 LEVEL 4: FLUENT READERS

Silver Dolphin Books
An imprint of Printers Row Publishing Group
A division of Readerlink Distribution Services, LLC
9717 Pacific Heights Blvd, San Diego, CA 92121
www.silverdolphinbooks.com

© 2021 Discovery or its subsidiaries and affiliates. Animal Planet and related logos are trademarks of Discovery or its subsidiaries and affiliates, used under license. All rights reserved.

AnimalPlanet.com

No part of this publication may be reproduced, distributed, or transmitted in any form or by any means, including photocopying, recording, or other electronic or mechanical methods, without the prior written permission of the publisher, except in the case of brief quotations embodied in critical reviews and certain other noncommercial uses permitted by copyright law.

Printers Row Publishing Group is a division of Readerlink Distribution Services, LLC.

Silver Dolphin Books is a registered trademark of Readerlink Distribution Services, LLC.

All notations of errors or omissions should be addressed to Silver Dolphin Books, Editorial Department, at the above address.

ISBN: 978-1-64517-935-1

Manufactured, printed, and assembled in Rawang, Selangor, Malaysia.

First printing, June 2021. THP/06/21

25 24 23 22 21 1 2 3 4 5

Hello! My name is Major.

I am the first dog to go from living in an **animal shelter** to living in the White House!

WASHINGTON D.C.

The White House is the home of the president of the United States. It's in our nation's capital, Washington, D.C.

Three years before I moved to the White House, I was just a newborn puppy. I had been born into a **litter** of six puppies. I had five sisters!

While we were still very young, we were left at an animal shelter.

The shelter staff noticed that something was wrong. My sisters and I were sick and weak.

The shelter staff rushed us to an animal hospital. The **veterinarian** said we had eaten something **toxic**. We were treated and began to feel better.

Back at the shelter, we got lots of care and attention every day.

There was bath time, cuddle time, and playtime, too!

The shelter found me the perfect family—the Biden family. They wanted to adopt me, but had to **foster** me first to make sure I was a good fit.

My foster dad, Joe, has loved dogs ever since he was a little boy.

Adoption Certificate

for: **MAJOR**

From the beginning, it was clear that we all loved each other. I grew big and strong under the Bidens' care.

It wasn't very long before they adopted me, and I became an official part of their family!

Two years later, my dad was **elected** president. That's when we moved to the White House.

A lot of important work happens at the White House.

There are tennis balls to fetch…

squirrels to chase…

and holes to dig!

My dad, Joe, has a lot of important work, too. But he always finds time for me.

We both like ice cream!

My mom, Jill, also works hard.

She's a teacher. She loves books, animals, and kids.

Guess what's the best part?
I have a big brother!

Meet Champ. He's not only my brother, he's my best friend.

I have a lot of energy and like to run around. Champ plays with me, but he likes to nap, too.

Champ and I are German Shepherds.

German Shepherds are a **breed** of dog. There are hundreds of different dog breeds.

German Shepherds are big, gentle dogs.

We are known for our loyalty and intelligence.

We're great **protectors**. We always look out for our families.

German Shepherds have an excellent sense of smell. We can smell things people—and many other dogs—cannot.

I can tell by my nose that there's a lot of history in my new home.

The White House is huge. It has one hundred and thirty-two rooms! That means there are a lot of places to play hide and seek.

There's even more room to play outside. The South Lawn is my favorite. It has big trees, green grass, and a fountain that makes a great swimming pool.

Watch me run on the South Lawn!

The Rose Garden is near the house. From there, I can peek inside the Oval Office. That's where my dad spends a lot of time.

If I bark "hello" loud enough, he can hear me. Woof!

Champ and I aren't the first dogs to live in the White House. Many former presidents had **canine** companions.

President Obama had two dogs, Bo and Sunny.

Spotty lived in the White House twice—
with two different presidents! She was
born there during George H.W. Bush's
presidency, and became the dog of his
son, George W. Bush.

She returned to the White House when
George W. Bush was elected president.

A lot of animals besides dogs have lived in the White House.

President Bill Clinton's black-and-white cat Socks received thousands of letters from kids.

President William Howard Taft's pet cow, Pauline, provided milk for him!

President Woodrow Wilson had a flock of sheep. They kept the White House lawn trim by eating the grass.

Nature-lover Teddy Roosevelt had more pets than any other president.

They included dogs, cats, horses, ducks, ponies, parrots, snakes, guinea pigs, rabbits, and a one-legged rooster.

As a White House dog, I am following in some large paws and hoofs that came before me.

My dad is calling me now. It's time to play fetch.

See you later!

Adopting a Shelter Pet

Adopting a pet is a big **commitment**. You are promising to take care of that pet for the rest of its life.

If you think your family is ready to adopt a pet, you should figure out what kind of pet is right for you.

Big dogs like Major and Champ need plenty of space. Some smaller dogs have a lot of energy and need to be walked and played with a lot. Can you give a pet what it needs to have a happy life? Do some research about what different kinds of pets need and also ask the shelter staff for advice. They are experts at matching people and pets.

At your local shelter, you'll find plenty of pets in need of loving homes. You may even find a new best friend!

Glossary

animal shelter: a temporary home for dogs, cats, and other animals, where they receive care until they are adopted

breed: a type of animal

canine: dog

commitment: a promise to do something

elected: chosen by votes

foster: to take care of a pet until it can be adopted

litter: a group of baby animals born at the same time

protector: one who guards something or someone

toxic: poison or other dangerous substance

veterinarian: an animal doctor